This Movie Will Require Dinosaurs

This
MOVIE
Will Require
DINOSAURS

C. W. Neill

A PERIGEE BOOK

A PERIGEE BOOK
Published by the Penguin Group
Penguin Group (USA) LLC
375 Hudson Street, New York, New York 10014

USA • Canada • UK • Ireland • Australia • New Zealand • India • South Africa • China

penguin.com

A Penguin Random House Company

THIS MOVIE WILL REQUIRE DINOSAURS

ISBN: 978-0-399-16770-6

An application to catalog this book has been submitted to the Library of Congress.

First edition: July 2014

PRINTED IN THE UNITED STATES OF AMERICA

10 9 8 7 6 5 4 3 2 1

Text design by Kristin del Rosario
Illustrations by Barak Hardley

Most Perigee books are available at special quantity discounts for bulk purchases for sales promotions, premiums,
fund-raising, or educational use. Special books, or book excerpts, can also be created to fit specific needs. For
details, write: Special.Markets@us.penguingroup.com.

INTRODUCTION

Hello. My name is C. W. Neill. Welcome to my book.

Now, you may be asking yourself, "Who the heck's this guy and why does he have a book?" Great question. I'll answer it now.

You see, as long as I can remember, I've always loved movies. I love the way they make me feel, I love the places they take me, I love the words the people say while they're in them. And as long as that love has existed, I've been coming up with movie ideas of my own. Like, *really* good movie ideas. I guess I just got lucky and have one of those imaginations that's never ending and capable of absolutely anything, ya know?

More recently, this has led to me trying to put these ideas on paper in what is called a "screenplay." It's like the written version of a movie, but it's not a book. Does that make sense? It's also called a "script" sometimes. You guys have heard of scripts before, right? That's what these are. But for the longest time no one ever heard my ideas or read my scripts.

Until now . . .

So one day, my best friend Randy was over at my place and we were just hanging out. Then he just happened to look at my computer and see what I was working on and he *literally lost his mind* over how good my ideas were. He was actually laughing hysterically out of amazement, even though they weren't comedies. He begged me to let him read some more, so I was just like, "OK, yeah. Go for it." Then he read like a hundred more and he loved every one of them. It was in that very moment that I thought, "OK, maybe you've got something here, C.W."

Then, sure enough, fourteen months later here we are! An entire book chockfull of some of my best and most interesting ideas. Incredible.

Now, keep in mind, these are only the very beginnings of my ideas. "Idea seeds," if you will. Seeds that will one day grow into huge idea trees that make millions of dollars at the box office and make certain people regret breaking up with me. Once I finish them, that is. But for now, it turns out just these very beginnings are already super-interesting and worth making a book out of.

So I guess that's it! I hope you like my book. I think it's pretty good.

Please, enjoy.

—C. W. Neill

INT. I DON'T KNOW, AN APARTMENT?

DAVE sits on the couch or whatever. Maybe he's standing, it doesn't
matter.

EXT. WAREHOUSE

Anywhere from twenty to twenty-five GUYS are involved in a gunfight.
Some of the guys are GOOD GUYS, some of them are BAD GUYS, and one
of them is AGENT JOHN MACKEY (good guy).

Mackey's a great shot, so he's just taking out Bad Guys one by one.
He shoots BAD GUY #7, but he doesn't die right away.

>   BAD GUY #7
>   If I'm going down, you're going down with me,
>   Mackey!

He pushes a red button on a DETONATOR and the whole place blows up
in flames. But not before Mackey and the remaining Good Guys get out
just in time.

>   AGENT JOHN MACKEY
>   Who wants tacos?

Stupid question. Everybody does.

INT. LOCKER ROOM

A bunch of SPORTS GUYS are hootin' and hollerin' because they just
won the big game.

COACH enters and blows his WHISTLE. The guys hush up real quick.
They don't know what he's gonna say.

                    COACH
          Cool sports, men. *Very* cool sports.

The guys all go back to celebrating, but now they're including Coach
and everyone's really enjoying themselves.

EXT. FIELD

There's a bunch of TREES. Right now I'm picturing SEQUOIA TREES. But depending on what kind of location we're able to get once production starts, that can change. Just know that sequoia trees are preferred.

A TYRANNOSAURUS REX shows up and he is *pissed*.

NOTE: This movie will require dinosaurs.

INT. OFFICE

DAN sits at his desk, hard at work on some WORK.

His assistant, MAGGIE, enters.

                    MAGGIE
          Here are those reports you asked for, Dan.

                    DAN
          Thank you, Maggie. Could you close the door for
          a moment, please?

Maggie closes the door and then Dan immediately starts grabbing her
BOOBS. She's clearly into it, so they start French-kissing and taking
off each other's CLOTHES in preparation for HOT SEX (hopefully).

EXT. THE PLAINS OF AVALON

TRIBERION rides his trusty steed YULU across the never ending PLAINS
OF AVALON.

Suddenly he hears the familiar cries of an EAGLE OF ARGLARD and
looks to the sky. Sure enough:

                    EAGLE OF ARGLARD
          Hey, Triberion, what's up?

                    TRIBERION
          Hey, dude.

EXT. PRISON YARD

A bunch of PRISONERS are playing BASKETBALL and lifting WEIGHTS and stabbing each other via SHANKS.

JASON STATHAM'S CHARACTER enters the yard and gets this squinty look on his face like, "Come on, sun, really?"

                    JASON STATHAM'S CHARACTER (V.O.)
          I never really thought of myself as the "prison
          type." But I guess when the United States
          government thinks you tried to kill the President,
          you don't get much say in the matter, do ya? Oh
          well... I voted for the other prick anyway.

Then he just starts punching EVERYBODY.

INT. CHANDLER AND JOEY'S APARTMENT

CHANDLER and JOEY are sitting in their RECLINERS watching TV.

ROSS enters with the biggest JAR OF MAYONNAISE you've ever seen in your life.

                    CHANDLER
        Uh... witty, sarcastic quip much?

                  STUDIO AUDIENCE
Hahahahahahahahahahahahahahahahaha.

Sports Movie Ideas

☆ - Babies that can dunk
  - "Air Babies"
 - "Babies In The Outfield"
 - ~~"Baby Ball"~~

Body Switching AND Sports!!!

- Like "A League Of Their Own" but for football.
   - NFFL: National Female Football League
  - based on a true story? (do research)
  - "Another League Of Their Own"
  - "A League Of Their Own 2: Football"

- wheelchair guys playing sports
   - "Wheelchairs In The Outfield"

INT. APARTMENT

MARY is breaking up with her boyfriend JASON. Jason isn't very happy
about the whole thing.

> MARY
> (crying)
> I'm sorry, it's just not working out.

> JASON
> What do you mean it's not working out?! That's
> bullshit and you know it! It's been working out
> for the last five years, hasn't it?

Mary just looks at the ground.

> JASON (CONT'D)
> This relationship has been working out for so
> long that it could compete in weight lifting
> competitions! Or maybe be a trainer or
> something. It's been working out for so long that
> when people pass it on the street they stop and
> think, "Jeez is that relationship on steroids?
> Look how strong it is." Because that's what
> happens when things work out for so long, Mary,
> they get REALLY FUCKING STRONG! And that's what
> happened with this relationship. It's gotten
> really, really strong because it's worked out for
> so long. And the fact that you're sitting there,
> trying to tell me that it's not working out...
> like some kind of fat, out of shape loser that
> doesn't take care of its body, is horse shit!
> How dare you sit there and say something like
> that to me. After all the working out we've done
> together...

Mary still doesn't say anything.

> JASON (CONT'D)
> Well, I guess that's it then. Looks like I won't
> have a spotter the next time I bench press my
> love for you.

INT. HEADQUARTERS

A bunch of important GUYS are sitting around a big round table and
they all look super-nervous.

THE PRESIDENT enters. Everyone sits up straight.

                    THE PRESIDENT
          All right, fellas, I need ideas and I need 'em
          now. What the heck are we gonna do about this
          Godzilla guy?!

All the important Guys just shrug like, "Beats me."

JOHN MCCLANE enters *dramatically.*

INT. BATHROOM

JULIE is getting ready for bed.

First she flosses. Then she brushes her teeth. Then she washes her face.

Then there's probably a couple minutes of girl stuff that I'm not really sure about. Then she poops. I think. Right?

INT. BAR - EVENING

TIM enters and starts scopin' the place out. It's straight up
crawling with CHICKS and they *all* got boobs. He smirks and nods
like, "Oh yeah, here we go."

Then he realizes that yet another sexual conquest won't fill the hole
in his heart and what he really wants more than anything is to be
loved. Truly loved.

Tim exits.

INT. KITCHEN

ROBIN is making DINNER, and she looks tired from a long day.

TROY enters, drops his BRIEFCASE by the front door, and walks into
the kitchen.

                    ROBIN
          Hey, sweetie!

                    TROY
          Hey, baby.

Then Troy walks up behind Robin and hugs her *sensually*. Robin makes
this face like, "Oh, that's nice." Then Troy reaches down her PANTS
and Robin makes this other face like, "HELLO."

EXT. BASEBALL FIELD

A group of YOUNG MEN are doing some casual BASEBALL. They're having a great time because they're friends and they love the game. Some things never change, know what I mean, haha.

Then, get this—THE APOCALYPSE starts happening. WHAT?! Ugh. So now the guys have to go help, but they don't have time to change. So they just wear their baseball outfits for the whole movie and they look really, really cool.

ATTN: POTENTIAL PRODUCERS AND/OR DIRECTORS: The baseball outfits are NONNEGOTIABLE, so don't even try it.

```
--------------
```

INT. SECRET HIDEOUT

AMY (29, the most beautiful woman in the world) is tied up in a
chair in the middle of the room. She's surrounded by HENCHMAN #1
(early 30s, Caucasian, average body type), HENCHMAN #2 (late 20s,
Caucasian, strong body type), and HENCHMAN #3 (late 30s, Caucasian,
strong body type).

Then, suddenly, AGENT JOHN MACKEY bursts in through the front door.
All the Henchmen are startled.

                    AGENT JOHN MACKEY
               (to Amy)
          Sorry I'm late, babe.

Amy tries to smile, but she can't because they punched her a bunch
and she is gagged.

                    HENCHMAN #1
          Get him!

They all rush toward Mackey to try to take him out, but they are
swiftly met with a series of punches and kicks, leaving them dead
and lifeless. Mackey walks over to Amy and takes the gag out of her
mouth.

                    AGENT JOHN MACKEY
          'Sup?

```
---------------
```

INT. HI-TECH SCIENCE LAB

DANIEL is running a few last-minute diagnostics before they test out
THE MACHINE. He looks very determined, while LINDA looks very
nervous.

> LINDA
> Listen, Daniel, I don't think this is such a
> good idea.

> DANIEL
> Neither do I, but I don't have a choice goddamn
> it! If I don't do this, the Lizard Man will keep
> killing innocent people! And he wouldn't even
> exist if it wasn't for us. We need to stop him.
> I need to stop him!

> LINDA
> You are so brave. I love you.

> DANIEL
> Shut the fuck up.

EXT. HOUSE - FRONT YARD

The house is huge. Two floors, a bunch of WINDOWS, and of course a
FRONT DOOR.

The front yard has a big TREE in the corner, and there is a SWING
tied to the thickest branch. It's really a beautiful sight. The
perfect house.

Then, out of nowhere, *a pack of ELEPHANTS runs past the house!* And
right after they've passed the title's like, BOOM:

"JUMANJI 2"

EXT. DRIVEWAY

A couple DUDES are hanging out dribbling BASKETBALLS.

Then this OTHER DUDE comes walking out of the house, and the first
two Dudes are like:

                    DUDES
          Hey, dude! Come dribble these basketballs
          with us!

And the Other Dude just smiles and says:

                    OTHER DUDE
          Honestly, dudes; you're like my best friends in
          the whole wide world and there is *nothing* I
          would love to do more than dribble those bas-
          ketballs with you.

Then the Other Dude joins the first two Dudes for some good ole-
fashioned ball dribblin' and they never talk about the murders ever
again.

INT. TORTURE ROOM

JAMES BOND is being tortured by DR. DEATHMAN. They call him that because he is known for killing people and he has a PhD.

                    DR. DEATHMAN
          Have you been experiencing any... *discomfort*?!

And right as he says "discomfort," he punches James in the face.

                    JAMES BOND
          Yes, dude! Every time you punch me! That really
          hurts! *Please stop doing that.*

Dr. Deathman makes a note on his chart.

INT. CAFE

SUSAN and BETH are sitting at a table talking about... last night's episode of *Sex in the City*? I don't know.

TIFFANY enters and looks around. Susan and Beth notice her and start waving like, "Hey, over here!" Tiffany sees them and she's like, "Oh, there you are." Then they start screaming a bunch and Tiffany gives both Susan and Beth individual hugs.

Nearby, a WAITRESS has this look on her face like, "I quit."

"Chain of command" (cool title)

War Movies

- war movies are pretty popular
- gotta be gory (blood, limbs, death, etc.)
- gotta have heroes/sacrifices
- what war hasn't gotten a movie yet?
    - Korean
    - Gulf? (research)

Period Pieces

☆- Elian Gonzales
    - not a war movie but still super interesting

- Has anyone made a movie about OJ getting away with that murder yet???

☆ WWSD: What Would Spielberg Do? ☆

Sunny Afternoon

what a beautiful afternoon,
out here in the warm sunlight.
Maybe later, I'll grab an ice cream cone.
I think I may, I think I just might.
At this exact moment, I have no fears,
no pain, no regrets.
At this exact moment, something, something,
something The New York Mets. (what?)

INT. AN OFFICE

I'm sitting opposite a large DESK and I have a very distinct JAWLINE.
You can't see who's sitting behind the desk yet as the CHAIR is
facing the window.

                    ME
          This better be good. It took me forever to get
          here from my mansion in Malibu, California.

The chair slowly spins around to reveal...

                    STEVEN SPIELBERG
          I've got three words for you... E. T. Two.

I think for a moment.

                    ME
          I'm in.

Then we shake hands and start laughing about how rich we're gonna
be, and I just can't wait to call Amy and tell her the good news
because I love her so much.

INT. CHURCH

All the KIDS are asleep, all the ADULTS are holding in farts, and all the OLD PEOPLE are not holding in farts.

The PREACHER is at the podium just gettin' his preach on. And it's goin good, man. People are listening *intently*. Except for this one guy, ERIC. But he's deaf. So, technically, he's never listened to anything.

> PREACHER
> Something about God... And also, some other
> stuff about Jesus...

REMINDER: Find out what preachers usually say.

EXT. DAYTONA 500

A bunch of RACE CARS are driving at least one hundred miles an hour while also making a significant number of left turns. And they're all having a great time doing it.

Then this OTHER RACE CAR shows up and he's like:

> OTHER RACE CAR
> I'mma make right turns.

And then everyone crashes and dies.

NOTE: This movie will be animated.

EXT. PARK

It's your average park in your average neighborhood. There's a
BASEBALL FIELD in one corner, a BASKETBALL COURT in another, and a
bunch of MEXICANS playing soccer in the middle.

Suddenly it gets very dark, almost as if something is blocking the
sun. All the Mexicans stop playing soccer and look up in awe.

It's ALIENS.

EXT. ROAD

JOHN MACKEY is speeding down the road in a big TRUCK, desperately
trying to keep up with a VAN full of ROBBERS (three). AMY (29,
somehow beautiful even when she's terrified) is sitting in the
passenger seat and she is terrified.

                         AMY
            Slow down! Slow down!

                    JOHN MACKEY
            Shut your goddamn mouth.

Amy is offended for a second, but then she realizes she likes being
told what to do, especially by John, so she does, in fact, shut her
goddamn mouth.

INT. RESTAURANT - EVENING

DANIEL and JAMIE sit at a table. They're on a date.

Daniel is trying to pretend that he's not thinking about having sex
with Jamie. Jamie is trying to pretend that she's not thinking about
how much she doesn't want to have sex with Daniel.

                    JAMIE
          So, what do you do?

                    DANIEL
          Probably something with math.

Jamie falls asleep.

INT. OFFICE

BRAD and KEVIN are goofing off again while everyone else is hard at work.

Nearby, CHRIS decides he's finally had enough of their behavior, so he stands up to go confront them. Then he remembers that he's a little punk bitch and he's terrified of confrontation. So he sits back down and decides to just not do anything about it for another fifteen goddamn years.

INT. BEDROOM

A YOUNG MAN (black) is doing some PUSH-UPS and he's really good at them. I bet he's done *at least* seventy. Then, finally, he stops. He's breathing really hard, probably because he just did *at least* seventy push-ups, and he's staring at something.

INSERT: A blurry picture of BLADE (Wesley Snipes) hangs on the wall.

> YOUNG MAN
> (ominously)
> See ya soon... *Dad.*

WHAAAAAAAAAAAAAAAAAAAAAAAAAAAAAAAAAAAAAAAAAAAAAAAAAAAAT?! No way.

EXT. BATTLEFIELD

The NORTH is getting ready to fight the SOUTH. It's the CIVIL WAR
(American).

GENERAL SUMNER rides out in front of the NORTH GUYS to address them
before they start killing and dying.

> GENERAL SUMNER
> OK, fellas, listen up. I know it's been a long,
> hard couple of years. And I know we've lost a
> lot of good men. Really good men. Some nice
> ones, some funny ones, some that could play
> instruments. They're all gone. Dead. And I know
> how much of a bummer that is, trust me. No one's
> as bummed as me. Probably 'cause I'm in charge
> and all that stuff kind of falls on me, I get
> that.
>> (beat)
> I know you're tired. I know you're hurtin'. But
> guys, those other dudes over there? Pretty sure
> they wanna kill you. Probably because they know
> if they don't kill you, you're gonna kill them.
> So how's about this? Let's get excited, let's get
> motivated! Let's find whatever little bit of
> energy we may have left and let's go take care
> of business! All right?! Who's with me?!

All the Guys are like, "Yeah, all right."

EXT. STREET

ROSS and JOEY are walking down the street. Joey is wearing a really
big SHIRT and Ross is wearing a WEIRD SWEATER.

CHANDLER approaches, and he is wearing a SHIRT that is even bigger
than Joey's big shirt.

Then RACHEL and MONICA and PHOEBE show up, and you can see all six
of their NIPPLES through their TANK TOPS.

Then they talk about something stupid.

EXT. STREET

A MAN sits on a BENCH. He looks like a totally normal guy just
waiting for the BUS, and there's no way he's an assassin.

PHIL approaches and sits on the opposite end of the bench. He barely
even notices the Man. And even if he did, he would just think he's a
normal guy and definitely not an assassin.

> MAN
> Phil Peterson?

> PHIL
> Uh, yeah. Do I know you?

> MAN
> No.

Then suddenly the Man *shoots Phil in the head with a GUN and he dies
right there of a gunshot wound to the head!* Oh man, that normal guy
was actually an assassin! What a development.

INT. FLIGHT SCHOOL — OFFICE

SOME GUY stamps a piece of PAPER.

> SOME GUY
> Congratulations, you're now a pilot.

> PICKLES THE TALKING DOG
> *WHO LET THE DOGS FLY?!*
> (pointing)
> You. You. You. You.

Hello, my name is Amy Neill.

Amy Elizabeth Neill
Mr. & Mrs. C.W. Neill
C.W. & Amy Neill

Super Hero Movies

★ Reminder: ask a nerd. ★

- which ones haven't been made yet?
- Gotta have a villain (super?)
- Make up your own!
    - Tigerman
    - The Bowling Ball
    - ~~Mr. Magnet~~
★ - Gun Hands, Mr. Gun Hands
    - The Badger
    - Badger man
    - Birdguy

other hands:

EXT. CAFE - MORNING

It's your average hole-in-the-wall cafe. One of those places that probably has really good sandwiches and when people talk about it they say, "Best Arnold Palmers in town."

TIFFANY and CHARLIE enter and sit at a table. A WAITER approaches.

                    WAITER
          Hi. Can I get you guys started with some
          drinks?

                    CHARLIE
          Yes. Can I get a glass of milk, please?

                    WAITER
          No. You're in your twenties.

EXT. LOS ANGELES INTERNATIONAL AIRPORT - ARRIVALS

Various TRAVELERS stand around waiting for their BROTHER or SISTER
or WIFE or HUSBAND or BOYFRIEND or GIRLFRIEND or ROOMMATE or JUST
FRIEND to come pick them up while a bunch of CARS are all over the
place.

Suddenly AMY (29, so beautiful even after a seven-hour flight) runs
out of the airport in a rush and bumps into an OLD GUY, spilling
SAUSAGES *everywhere*.

EXT. BACKYARD

Five GUYS are hangin' in the backyard just gettin' their GRILL on
and throwing the PIGSKIN around. Just another average Saturday
afternoon for these best buds!

Then, suddenly, the SKY turns gray and the weather changes
dramatically. The Guys just look at each other; they know what to
do. They all put on their RINGS OF POWER and fly up into the sky to
yet again defend Earth from the evil LORD WEATHERGUY (temp name).

EXT. BASEBALL FIELD

It's another beautiful day at the ole ballpark. The SUN is shining, the GRASS is green, and the DIRT is as brown as ever.

JOSH is pitching for the Bulldogs and it's going pretty bad. His teammates try to encourage him, but it doesn't matter. He's a belly-itcher. Plain and simple.

LEVI, the Tigers' best hitter and the reigning home run champ, steps up to the plate.

                    JOSH
          Pass.

EXT. STREET - NIGHT

SHANNON and CHAD are Frenching real hard.

Chad slowly reaches for Shannon's boob and *omg she totally lets him.*

I guess it's true what they say, Chad's da man.

INT. ABANDONED FACTORY

AGENT JOHN MACKEY is pinned behind a SOMETHING. He's taking fire from
every angle. AMY is starting to panic (but still looks gorgeous) as
she huddles in the corner next to John.

                    AMY
          There's six of them, John! What are we
          gonna do?!

John checks the clip of his gun.

                    JOHN MACKEY
          Good thing I've got six bullets left.

John spins around and fires a shot up and to the left. Boom. THE
BLACK ONE's dead. Then he lowers his aim and fires another shot.
Boom. You're gone, CRAZY HAIRCUT GUY. Then he tumbles over some
PIPES and takes another shot. Thanks for playing, STONE COLD STEVE
AUSTIN. Then he whips around to his right and fires another shot.
SUNGLASSES GUY is out of the picture. Then he puts the gun behind
his back to take out ASIAN TONY DANZA. Then he does another full
spin and shoots EYE PATCH GUY right through his one remaining
EYEBALL. He did it. Amazing.

Amy runs up to John and starts hugging and kissing him. John plays
it really cool 'cause that's just who he is. But he totally knows
they're about to have hot sex.

EXT. LAKE

It's a beautiful day at the lake, and plenty of people have come out
to enjoy some fun in the sun. Some people are SKIING, some people
are INNER TUBING, and some people (ideally women) are just catchin'
some rays and working on their TAN.

Then a BRONTOSAURUS shows up and starts drinking from the lake and
everyone's like, "Holy cow, look at that brontosaurus!"

NOTE: This movie will require dinosaurs.

INT. DOLLAR STORE

It's a pretty cool store. Everything only costs a DOLLAR.

TRAVIS enters and approaches an EMPLOYEE.

>   TRAVIS
> Excuse me, does everything really only cost one
> dollar?

>   EMPLOYEE
> Yes, sir.

>   TRAVIS
> But I have, like, thirty dollars.

>   EMPLOYEE
> Well, then you could buy thirty things.

Then Travis literally loses his mind and spends the rest of his life
in a MENTAL INSTITUTION.

EXT. ROUTE 66

JASON STATHAM (ideally) is walking down the side of the road. He's wearing a really cool TRENCH COAT and carrying a GUITAR CASE as he walks down the side of the road.

In the distance he sees a CAR approaching. A car? In 2037? This should be interesting. As it gets closer to him, it slows down and comes to a stop. Then the driver takes off his sunglasses, and it's KAREEM ABDUL-JABBAR (ideally).

                    KAREEM ABDUL-JABBAR
          Where do you think you're going, Agent Zero?

                    JASON STATHAM
          With all due respect, Mr. President, that's none
          of your damn business.

EXT. STREET — DAY

AGENT REYNOLDS chases an INTERNATIONAL CRIMINAL through the busy
streets of MILWAUKEE, WISCONSIN. The International Criminal can
totally tell that Reynolds is the best agent in THE BUREAU, and ever
since his WIFE was brutally murdered there's no stopping him.

So he pulls out a THING and pushes a BUTTON, and just like that, *he
vanishes into thin air.* Reynolds is shocked, but keeps his wits.

                    AGENT REYNOLDS
          International criminal...?

EXTREME CLOSE-UP:

                    AGENT REYNOLDS
          More like inter-*dimensional* criminal!

Oh yeah, also, this movie is set in the future.

EXT. STREET

AMY (29, disgusting and covered in dirt) sits on the sidewalk in a
pile of GARBAGE that is now her house because her whole life has
fallen apart ever since she made the mistake of breaking up with me.

EXT. MAJOR CITY - I'M THINKING CHICAGO

There are a bunch of BUILDINGS of various sizes, but most of them
have been destroyed on account of the Apocalypse that just happened.
Also there are some CARS that have been burned and the streets are
covered in DEBRIS and BODIES.

                    JOHN STONE (V.O.)
          March 17, 2007. Oprah is dead.

INT. CHURCH

FAMILY AND FRIENDS have gathered to honor the memory of JERRY because he is dead and this is his FUNERAL.

His best friend and band mate WILL delivers his eulogy.

>   WILL
>   A great man once said, "Don't stop believin'."
>   And that's what Jerry did. He never stopped
>   believin'. He never stopped believin' that he
>   could be one of the greatest guitar players the
>   world had ever seen. And he never stopped
>   believin' that he could beat cancer. Unfortunately
>   for him, and all of us, God did not share those
>   beliefs.
>   (beat)
>   Jerry was a great man, and a great musician.
>   The best I've ever jammed with. Any way you want
>   it, that's the way you'd get it. And he would
>   give it to you, faithfully. As long as that
>   wheel in the sky kept on turnin', he kept on
>   rockin'. And now he's gone. Gone forever. No
>   more lovin', touchin', squeezin'. No more open
>   arms. Only memories. Good memories, happy
>   memories. Goodbye, old friend. It was quite a
>   Journey. This one's for you.

Then Will picks up a guitar and proceeds to sing Steve Perry's "Oh Sherrie" but says "Jerry" instead of "Sherrie."

VELOCICOPPERS

- "Lethal Weapon" meets "Dinosaurs" the TV show

- Are there humans?
    - maybe one human cop accidentally goes back in time & has to help the Velocicoppers solve a big crime.

really good →

- Do they have guns?
- Do they have cop cars?   > Yes.
- Do they like doughnuts?

- Whats the main conflict? What kinds of crimes happened in the Dinosaur times?
    - probably lots of murder
        - carniverous in nature
    - Drugs? Weed was totally around
    - Money? Do they have banks?
        ☆ - Dinosaur bank robbers ☆

The Robbersaurus's

↑ really really good

INT. RUSSELL CROWE'S HOUSE

RUSSELL CROWE is hosting another one of his infamous Hollywood
parties. Everyone's there: TOM CRUISE, REBECCA ROMIJN, JOHN CENA,
CLINT EASTWOOD, JON BON JOVI, and even WILMER VALDERRAMA.

I enter with my current girlfriend, YASMINE BLEETH. She looks
amazing and I have really clear skin. Everyone's all like, "Aw yeah,
here we go!" Because now that I'm there the party can *really* start.

EXT. PUBLIC POOL

BRODY (early 20s, Caucasian, strong body type) sits atop the LIFEGUARD
TOWER as he is the LIFEGUARD. He looks absolutely amazing. His HAIR?
Flawless. His SKIN? Golden *and* glistening. His PECS and BICEPS and
ABS? The definition of definition. Women want him, men want to be him.

Then, suddenly, a PERSON starts to drown, but Brody is too busy
glistening, so he doesn't notice, and they die :(

INT. AIRPORT HANGAR

Some MILITARY GUYS are getting ready for the big mission.

Everybody's there: TOO TALL, DAKOTA PETE, HORSE FACE, CAPTAIN
MUSCLES, HAYSTACK, MR. MUSCLES, JACK RABBIT, BULLET GUY, KNIFE MAN,
PICKLES, CARL THE MURDERER, DR. DENIM, CHUD, CEILING FAN, TURKEY
SANDWICH, PROFESSOR BROWN PANTS, UGGO, SOUR DOUG, THE POOP NAZI,
COTTON CANDY, DIP SHIT, SHIT DIP, CHICKEN TENDER, CODE RED MOUNTAIN
DREW, LAMP SHADE, TWEEDLEDEE, TWEEDLEDUM, TWEEDLESMART, PEANUT
BUTTER, JELLY, PUKE MOUTH, BORING STEVE, HOLD THE GUAC, DUMP TRUCK,
FLAPJACK, NO TEETH, TOO MANY TEETH, THREE BALLS, TIPTOE, DICK CHEESE,
ARMPIT, BLINDY, BANANA FRANK, FILIPINO PHILLIP, and of course, JON
BON JOVI (ideally).

                    JON BON JOVI
          All right, fellas. Just remember—if you're
          gonna go down, go down in a BLAZE OF GLORY!

                    EVERYONE
          Oh my god/Really, dude?/Shut the fuck up, Bon
          Jovi.

INT. LIVING ROOM

JESSICA and LAUREN are having a girls' night. And let me tell ya
what, they are really lettin' loose. They got ICE CREAM, they got
NAIL POLISH, they got TAMPONS (right?). And of course they're
watching their favorite movie, *Miss Congeniality 2*.

Then JACKIE enters with three BOTTLES OF WINE, and they all
literally scream for twenty seconds followed by FRENCH BRAIDS.

EXT. SPACE

WARPMAN and DR. ELEMENT are engaged in a heated SPACE FIGHT. Gravity doesn't exist in space, so every blow is multiplied by one thousand, and if you bleed, the BLOOD just kind of floats around. Needless to say, it's a pretty cool space fight.

Dr. Element pulls a piece of TECTONIC out of his POCKET.

                    WARPMAN
          How?! It was all destroyed!

                    DR. ELEMENT
          You would think that!

Then he throws the Tectonic at Warpman, but Warpman has great reflexes, so he quickly catches it and throws it right back at Dr. Element, hitting him square in the chest and causing him to burst into *nothingness*.

                    WARPMAN
               (super-cool)
          You would die like that.

INT. BASKETBALL ARENA

It's the Championship Game and emotions are high. The place is
packed to the brim with FANS, and they're all on their FEET as
there's only four seconds left. BULLDOGS' ball, down two; if they
don't score, THE MUSTANGS win the Championship. Emotions are high.
Four seconds left. Championship Game.

JOHNNY inbounds the ball to DERRICK. He dribbles the BASKETBALL
three times and throws up a 3-pointer. If it goes in, they win the
game. The Championship Game. Emotions are high.

BEGIN SLOW-MOTION SEQUENCE:

Cut back and forth between:

-The ball flying through the air.

-Derrick watching the ball fly through the air.

-The ball flying through the air.

-MUSTANG #2 watching the ball fly through the air.

-The ball flying through the air.

-DERRICK'S MOM covering her eyes because she just can't watch the
ball fly through the air.

-The ball flying through the air.

-COACH pulling his HAIR out as he watches the ball fly through the
air.

-The ball hits the RIM and bounces straight up.

-Derrick winces and leans as if to physically will the ball into the
HOOP.

-The ball comes back down and indeed goes IN THE HOOP!

The Bulldogs win the game! AMAZING!!! Everybody starts jumping up
and down and hugging each other. After all they've been through,
they actually pulled it off. What an unbelievable accomplishment by
such a ragtag group of fucking dumb pieces of shit.

INT. CAFE

A handful of PATRONS sit at various TABLES drinking COFFEE and
eating BUNDT CAKE(?).

One patron in particular is named KATE and she has great BOOBS.
Like, probably perfect boobs. I mean they're covered by a SHIRT and
probably some kind of BRA, but you can just tell. They gotta be
awesome. It just makes you think about the handful of lucky DUDES
that have gotten to look at them and squeeze them, ya know? They're
so cool.

STACY enters and her BOOBS are just average but whatever who cares
look at Kate.

EXT. NEW YORK CITY

The streets are full of PEOPLE walking to and from places. Most of them without a care in the world. Little do they know, the STATUE OF LIBERTY is about to blow up.

Suddenly, the Statue of Liberty *blows up*.

INT. HEADQUARTERS - CONTINUOUS

DR. JERMAINE looks out the window at the Statue of Liberty blowing up.

                    DR. JERMAINE
          They're here.

ALIENS.

INT. STARBUCKS

AMY (29, beautiful even at work) walks behind the register with a
clipboard taking notes and checking in on her EMPLOYEES. She looks
happy and, honestly, I'm happy for her. Things are going well for her
these days. She's been promoted, she started painting again, and she
hasn't had to hear my "incessant clicking" for over a year now so
congratufuckinglations GOOD FOR YOU I'M GLAD YOU GOT EXACTLY WHAT
YOU WANTED!!!

INT. BREAK ROOM

A small group of EMPLOYEES are on their lunch break. They eat in
silence. Probably because they're miserable and they hate their lives.

EVAN enters and he looks especially miserable. He's wearing a SUIT
that is way too big for him and his hair is all wrong and he has a
stupid GOATEE on his chin. He's only 32, but his eyes make him look
52, and you can just tell he's so lonely.

THE BOSS enters.

                    THE BOSS
          Oh hey, Evan, you're fired.

                    EVAN
          Cool. No problem.

Evan exits.

Influences/People I'd Like To Work With
- Statham ☆
- Any cast member from "Friends"
- Bruce
- Cruise
- Stiller (Ben only)
- Yasmine Bleeth
- Kutcher
- Eastwood
- Michael Bay
- John Woo
- Spielberg
- Anyone

Hey, I'm Amy and I suck and I'm stupid.

What's The Point Of This
What's the point of this?
What's the point of that?
What's the point of dogs?
What's the point of cats?
What's the point of me?
What's the point of you?
What's the point of anything?
What's your point of view? (stupid)

INT. LIVING ROOM

I enter, clearly beat from a long day at the office. I flop onto the
COUCH and let out a long, deep sigh.

Then my beautiful wife YASMINE BLEETH enters wearing nothing but an
APRON and I'm all like, "schwing!" (I get a boner.)

INT. CENTRAL PERK

The GANG enters and takes their usual seats. They sit in somber
silence as they've just come from JOEY'S FUNERAL.

GUNTHER walks over to take their orders.

                    GUNTHER
          Hey, where's Joey?

                    ROSS
          Gunther, you're a real fuckin' piece of shit,
          you know that?

                    GUNTHER
          Yeah...

Gunther hangs his head and walks away.

THIS MOVIE WILL REQUIRE DINOSAURS

INT. LOCKER ROOM

THE BRIDGEFIELD FIGHTING MEXICANS sit quietly on some BENCHES. They're minutes away from the biggest basketball game of their gosh darn lives.

COACH enters. Everyone sits up straight. For a few moments he just stares at them individually. I'd say like two to three moments per player. Then he starts talking *sternly* (as coaches typically do, think typical coach style).

                    COACH
          Listen up, men. In a few minutes you're gonna go
          out there and you're gonna play in the biggest
          basketball game of your gosh darn lives. Now,
          there's two ways this could go. One—you leave
          your heart and soul and blood and tears out
          there on that court and go home winners and
          champions. Or two—you act like a bunch of
          fartin' butt heads and play like dummies and lose
          and go home losers. Now, you have the ability to
          pull this off, I know you do. But you gotta make
          a choice, right here, right now. Do you wanna go
          out there and leave your heart and soul and
          blood and tears on the court and go home
          winners and champions? Or do you wanna act like
          a bunch of fartin' butt heads and play like
          dummies and lose and go home losers?
               (beat)
          What's it gonna be?

                    BILLY
          Sorry, what? I wasn't listening.

INT. BAR

A bunch of GUYS and GIRLS stand around screaming at each other and drinking SHITTY BEER.

The walls are decorated with really funny personalized LICENSE PLATES, like "BUTTMAN" and "BOOBGUY." And there are all kinds of sports playing on the bar's fifty-seven TVs.

KEN GRIFFEY JR. enters.

INT. BEDROOM

ROY and THERESA burst through the door and they are just going at
it. They have their MOUTHS open really wide and they're touching
TONGUES while they rip off each other's CLOTHES and it is hot.

Then Theresa reaches down Roy's PANTS and she makes the face like,
"whoa!" because she's pleasantly surprised by how big his WIENER is.
Roy's just like, "Yeah, I know."

INT. OFFICE

BRAD and KEVIN are hanging out in the CONFERENCE ROOM just goofing
off like idiots. They're drinking all the COCA-COLA that is supposed
to be for CLIENTS and paying no attention whatsoever to their actual
work.

Suddenly a PTERODACTYL shows up at the WINDOW and breaks through the
GLASS and grabs them and just immediately drops them to their
horrific DEATHS.

NOTE: This movie will require dinosaurs.

INT. DEPARTMENT STORE

WENDY and ANDREA are browsing the Women's Section at their favorite
department store while having a discussion about their boyfriends.

> WENDY
> Oh my god, my boyfriend is such a lazy slob!
> What about yours?

> ANDREA
> Oh yeah, such a slob. *And!* A jerk.

> WENDY
> Ugh, boyfriends...

Then they get FROYO.

EXT. ROAD

FRED is driving down the road in his 1997 NISSAN ALTIMA and he is wearing SHADES.

Then, out of nowhere, a STRANGE MAN runs across the road and Fred has to swerve to avoid hitting him. But in doing so he hits a 1984 FORD F-150 head on. Then the F-150 is rear-ended by a 2009 TOYOTA PRIUS which is then rear-ended by a 2003 TOYOTA CAMRY which is then rear-ended by a 1995 ISUZU RODEO which is then rear-ended by a 2004 SUBARU BAJA which is then rear-ended by a 1992 CHEVY SUBURBAN which is then rear-ended by a 2003 HONDA ACCORD which is then rear-ended by a MOTORCYCLE, causing the driver to fly over the Accord and hit the back of the Suburban and then all the cars catch on fire and EXPLODE. Killing most, if not all, of the drivers.

Fred vows to find the Strange Man and exact his revenge.

NOTE: Yes, it HAS to be those exact cars.

EXT. MOUNT ESTERIOUS

TRIBERION, weary and beaten, finally reaches the peak of MOUNT
ESTERIOUS. The first human to ever do so. He uses his remaining
strength to rise to his feet and lets out the CRY OF THE GODS, then
quickly falls to his knees, exhausted.

After a few moments, the CLOUDS begin to part and the SUN shines
down on him. He puts his hand up to block its harmful rays from his
BEAUTIFUL FACE. Then, suddenly—

                    THE VOICE OF HARFLON, GOD OF TRUTH
          Oh my god, *what?!* I'm busy.

EXT. MAJOR CITY

A violent storm is brewing. CITIZENS look up in fear.

INT. HEAVEN - CONTINUOUS

GOD is drunk and listening to Dashboard Confessional again.

Steve Carell is... Rip Van Winkle!

Other fairy tales
to make movies
out of???

Cool Lines

- "Time to die, guy."
- "I've got a bullet with your name on it."
    - (actually possible?)
- "I hope you can smell what The Rock is cooking. CAUSE ITS YOU."
    - (The Rock as a villain. Interesting...)
- "X,Y,Z ya later." (Dang!)
- "Roses are red, violets are blue. My wife is dead, and so are you." (bang!)
- "If you can't stand the heat, get out of hell."
- "ring, ring! It's for you." (punch!)
- "Who ordered the knuckle sandwich?" (punch!) "On wheat." (drops piece of wheat bread on guy)

☆ Reminder: Find out where Jason Statham lives ☆

EXT. MY MANSION - THE FUTURE

I'm sitting in my ROCKING CHAIR on the front porch of my mansion drinking LEMONADE, looking amazing for my age and being rich as fuck.

AMY (47, hasn't aged well at all) walks up. She's desperate and broke and lonely and wants me to take her back after all these years now that I'm rich and successful. But I don't even recognize her. And even if I did, she looks super-gross now, so I wouldn't even be interested.

Then I have SECURITY escort her off the premises and I go back to enjoying my *amazing* life.

INT. POOL HALL

Some BAD BOYS (five) are shooting POOL and smoking CIGARETTES.
They're all wearing WHITE T-SHIRTS and BLUE JEANS and they all have
BAD ATTITUDES.

                    BAD BOY #1
          Hey, what do you guys think about rules?

                    THE REST OF THE BAD BOYS
          Ugh!/Hate 'em!/They're not for me.

                    BAD BOY #1
          Yeah, me too!

Then they all comb their HAIR and start singing "Rules Are for
Fools."

Oh, this is a musical, by the way.

EXT. THE SURFACE OF MARS

ROBERTS and KELLY are out on their daily perimeter check. Suddenly, Roberts notices something moving on the horizon.

                    ROBERTS
          Whoa. Did you see that?

                    KELLY
          See what?

Suddenly a GIANT MONSTER THING shows up and rips Kelly's HEAD right off his BODY.

                    ROBERTS
          Oh, it was a giant monster thi—.

Then the Giant Monster Thing removes Roberts's HEAD as well.

INT. SUBWAY

The subway is full of PEOPLE of all different shapes and sizes and colors and smells.

SUZY enters and she looks really nice. Like, she seems like a person you could really trust, you know? She's not like, drop-dead gorgeous, but she's definitely not unattractive either. She's just an attractive woman that I could totally see myself marrying someday and she has welcoming EYES.

Then a HOMELESS MAN throws up *everywhere*.

INT. LIVING ROOM

ROGER and SUSAN are enjoying a quiet night in with a good movie and
a BOWL OF POPCORN.

Suddenly three MEN IN BLACK (not like *Men in Black*, just guys
wearing black) burst in the door and point their GUNS at Roger and
Amy demanding all of their valuables. But Roger is a real man and he
wouldn't let anything happen to his woman. So he throws the popcorn
in their faces and takes all of their guns in one motion. The Men in
Black are so surprised and scared they run away like little sissy
children.

                    SUSAN
          My god, you're incredible.

                    ROGER
          No doy.

EXT. STREET

ROSCOE and JACKSON are casually walking down the street drinking
COFFEE and eating DOUGHNUTS. They're laughing and smiling because
they're not only partners, they're pals.

BOOM! The bank they're walking past *explodes*, sending Roscoe and
Jackson into the street and a bunch of MONEY into the air. Nearby
CITIZENS begin frantically grasping at the money, but Roscoe and
Jackson just look at each other. They already know...

                    ROSCOE   JACKSON
              Alligator Pete...   Alligator Pete...

EXT. OLD WEST TOWN

Various TOWNSFOLK are doing Old West stuff like riding horses, sweeping porches, and being really, really depressed.

Just then DANGEROUS DAVE rides into town. He looks super-cool. His hair, his clothes, everything. But he's the bad guy. So [HERO'S NAME] is probably gonna kill him in the end. It'll be a good movie though, trust me.

EXT. PACIFIC COAST HIGHWAY

I'm driving down the road in my vintage '65 FORD MUSTANG with my
beautiful girlfriend, YASMINE BLEETH, at my side. I'm wearing cool
sunglasses and my hair looks great and I do not have scoliosis.

INT. ART SCHOOL - CLASSROOM

AMY (29, super-average-looking) enters and sits down in a chair.
She's nervous as this is her very first art class.

PROFESSOR WHATEVER enters.

                    PROFESSOR WHATEVER
          Hello, class, I'm Professor Whatever. Welcome to
          Art 101. For those of you that used this class
          as an excuse to break up with your boyfriend
          who wants nothing more in the world than to
          love you and make you happy—how can you live
          with yourself?

EXT. MIAMI INTERNATIONAL AIRPORT

Tired, and very much in need of a shower, BRIAN exits the airport
and is immediately startled by a grinning WILL SMITH.

                    WILL SMITH
          Welcome to Miami.

Will Smith hands Brian a copy of BAD BOYS II.

★CARS! More stuff with cool cars.
Everybody loves cool cars.

- what do people want to see ???
        - Explosions
        - Sex
Never underestimate - Heroes (male & female)
the impact of - Aliens/Zombies/Monsters
a great - Heists (cleverly executed)
soundtrack! - Lovable losers with hot chicks
        - Skilled hand to hand combat
        - Kids (MUST be cute and/or funny)

For My Love
Your smile warms my heart,
Your laughter speaks to my soul.
You are my life, my world, my everything.
    I will love you until the end of time.
So it sucks pretty hard that you dumped me.

```
---------------
```

EXT. STREET - NIGHT

Hundreds of YOUNG PEOPLE, most of them ASIAN, line the road while
cheering and doing drugs. In the middle of the road, two CARS are
in position to street race. They both look super-awesome, which is
to be expected as outward appearance is very important in the world
of street racing.

Suddenly three VELOCIRAPTORS show up and start eating some of the
young Asian people.

NOTE: This movie will require dinosaurs.

INT. CENTRAL PERK

ROSS and RACHEL enter and they are in a fight.

>   RACHEL
>   I can't believe you would do that!

>   ROSS
>   Excuse me?! I can't believe *you* would do *that!*

>   GUNTHER
>   (under his breath)
>   I can't believe *she* would do *you*.

Then Ross just starts beating the shit out of Gunther.

EXT. BACKYARD

A bunch of 20-SOMETHINGS have gathered for a HOUSE PARTY. Everyone is drinking DRINKS and smoking DRUGS and trying as hard as they can to eventually have SEX. Needless to say this party is so far off the hook it doesn't even know where the hook is anymore.

Then all of a sudden THE COPS show up and they're like:

> COPS
> Everyone FREEZE! You're under arrest for partying too hard!

But all the PARTY PEOPLE are just like:

> PARTY PEOPLE
> Shut up, no we're not.

So the Cops are like:

> COPS
> Dang it. OK.

And then they put their GUNS down and start partying, and now the hook is just long gone.

```
--------------
```

INT. THE CAVE OF DESPAIR

OSTERIUS enters the cave, ever so carefully, sword drawn. He knows full well the evils that live within such dark and scary places. He won't be fooled again.

Suddenly from the depths appears THE DRAGON. His giant, fiery EYES are an unfortunate and familiar sight to our hero.

Osterius pulls at his SHIRT COLLAR with his RIGHT HAND and makes this face like, "eeeeeyyyikes."

INT. KITCHEN

DERRICK is making some PASTA. Suddenly he realizes something—

DERRICK
Well, this is just too much pasta.

Then he realizes that he can just save some for lunch tomorrow and he nods like, "Good thinking, Derrick."

Then he realizes how completely meaningless his life is.

INT. BEDROOM

CHRIS and JULIE are lying in BED cuddling. Chris has his RIGHT ARM
around Julie and he's touching her BOOB and it's cool (the boob).

Then, out of nowhere, Chris rips a MONSTER FART and it's awesome (the
fart) but Julie's like:

                    JULIE
          Ugh, GROSS!

So Chris is like:

                    CHRIS
          Whatever, *you're* gross. Get your boob outta my
          hand.

Then they get in a fight and decide to call it off (the wedding).

- - - - - - - - - - - - - -

INT. BATHROOM

TRAVIS (28, a grown adult man) stands in front of the mirror trying
to shave, but he keeps screwing up and cutting himself.

> TRAVIS
> Man, I sure do wish my father would have taught
> me how to shave.
> > (beat)
> I wish he would have taught me a lot of
> things...

Then Travis tries to cry, but he can't because his father never told
him it was OK for a man to cry sometimes, *which it is*.

INT. HOUSE

OK, so it's a murder scene. There are some FORENSIC GUYS walking
around doing science stuff. There's also some REGULAR COPS taking
notes and drinking coffee. Plus there's a DEAD BODY on the floor and
it's gross.

ACE VENTURA enters in a nice SUIT and a good HAIRCUT. Everyone stops
what they're doing and looks at him.

                          ACE VENTURA
              All right then... what do we got?

And then the title's like BOOM:

"ACE VENTURA: REGULAR DETECTIVE"

EXT. STREET

BRAD and KEVIN are walking down the street. They just got off WORK, where they didn't actually do any work, and now they're probably going to meet some DUMB SLUTS at a STUPID BAR.

Then a TYRANNOSAURUS REX shows up out of *nowhere* and eats them both in one quick bite. EVERYONE ELSE starts to panic, but the Tyrannosaurus Rex has this look on his face like, "Nah, don't worry about it, I'm full now."

NOTE: This movie will require dinosaurs.

INT. MY SUBCONSCIOUS

There are mozzarella sticks *everywhere*.

EXT. GOLF COURSE

THE GUYS are enjoying some well-deserved HOLES (eighteen to be
exact). It's something they like to do at least once a week. They
just love getting outdoors, taking in some fresh air, and engaging
in some "friendly" competition—haha yeah right.

Not to mention, their KIDS are morons and their WIVES don't ever
shut the hell up.

So... Golf.

VELOCICOPPERS MOCK-UPS
"SCALES"

"Dinosaurs" style   "Jurrasic Park" style

"Hornsby"

Hornsby & Scales

EXT. BUILDING

ROSCOE and JACKSON run out of the building and take cover behind a
GARBAGE TRUCK.

                      ROSCOE
             See ya later, alligator.

He flips the switch on a DETONATOR and the building they just ran out
of *explodes to Kingdom Come.*

Once the dust clears, Roscoe and Jackson look at each other for a
few seconds and then say:

                JACKSON   ROSCOE
        In a while, crocodile!   In a while, crocodile!

Then they laugh uncontrollably for three minutes.

EXT. HOT TUB

I'm sitting in a hot tub with five BEAUTIFUL FRENCH MODELS. None of them are wearing their BIKINI TOPS and I have the perfect amount of CHEST HAIR. It's super-hot and wild and sexy, and I have a BONER, and it would have never happened if I was still dating Amy.

THANK GOD THAT'S OVER.

EXT. SECTOR 43 - PLANET Z

TEMPLETON and RUIZ carefully walk through SECTOR 43, which is a
FOREST ENVIRONMENT full of weird PLANTS and TWO-HEADED BIRDS because
this is an ALIEN PLANET.

Suddenly, they hear something rustling behind a PURPLE BUSH. They
turn, LASERS drawn, ready to defend themselves. Then, out of the
bushes, appears this really tall ALIEN LADY and she has three BOOBS
and they're huge. TEMPLETON's all like:

                    TEMPLETON
          Whoa...

But Ruiz is like:

                    RUIZ
          Ugh, gimme a break.

Ruiz is a woman.

INT. BAD GUY PLACE

All the BAD GUYS are hanging out doing bad guy stuff like running with SCISSORS, sitting too close to the TV, and taking the Lord's name in vain.

Suddenly the GOOD GUY bursts through the door and he's like:

                    THE GOOD GUY
          Freeze, you bad guys!

And the Bad Guys are like:

                    THE BAD GUYS
          Uh... *no.*

And then they just go right back to doing their bad guy stuff. So the Good Guy's like:

                    THE GOOD GUY
          Dang it. All right.

And he leaves.

INT. DANCE HALL

All the SEXY GIRLS are dropping their BUTTS to the floor and all the
FELLAS are going "aye yai *yai.*"

This one girl, FELICIA, has such a juicy butt that BRAD just can't
control himself and he starts grabbing for it like, "gimme gimme
gimme." But Felicia's all like, "nuh uh," and she does that Dikembe
Mutombo finger thing.

Overall, Brad's disappointed but he gets it. As much as he wanted to
touch Felicia's butt, he respects her for not letting him. Plus
there's plenty of other available butts.

INT. A PLACE

MAIN CHARACTER (age, brief description) enters. He seems pretty
upset.

                    MAIN CHARACTER
          ANGER! FRUSTRATION!

COMIC RELIEF (age, brief description) pops up from behind a THING.

                    COMIC RELIEF
          Uh, excuse me, something witty.

Main Character is so startled he drops all of his BAGUETTES.

INT. MY PANTS

The party is in full swing.

INT. OFFICE

RON sits at his desk, finishing up a REPORT. Once he's done, he leans back in his chair and lets out a sigh of relief.

Then he looks at the clock—9:24 A.M. He just shrugs and says:

                    RON
          Welp, that's Mondays for ya.

Then he cries for like twenty minutes.

INT. CLASSROOM

A bunch of rambunctious TEENAGERS are waiting for class to start. They clearly have no respect for authority, as they are throwing PAPER AIRPLANES, blowing BUBBLES with their BUBBLE GUM, and drawing WIENERS on their DESKS.

MR. B enters and he is BLACK and hopefully SAMUEL L. JACKSON.

> PUNK KID
> Who the hell are you?

Mr. B just punches the kid right in his STUPID UGLY FACE. Everyone is shocked.

> MR. B
> My name is Mr. B. I'm ya mothafuckin' substitute teacher.
> (beat)
> Any other questions?

EXT. STREET

Best gal pals JESS and MANDY are walking down the street getting in
some good exercise and even a few laughs while they're at it.

Up ahead they spot these two HOT GUYS headed their way and they get
real excited and start thinking about what their WIENERS might look
like (right?).

1. Alabama	26. New York
2. Arkansas	27. New Jersey
3. Alaska	28. New Hampshire
4. Arizona	29. Nevada
5. Colorado	30. Oregon
6. California	31. Ohio
7. Connecticut	32. Oklahoma
8. South Dakota	33. Pennsylvania
9. North Dakota	34. Rhode Island
10. Georgia	35. Texas
11. Delaware	36. Virginia
12. Indiana	37. Vermont
13. Idaho	38. Washington
14. Iowa	39. Wisconsin
15. Illinois	40. Florida
16. Kansas	41. New Mexico
17. Kentucky	42. Missouri
18. Louisiana	43. ~~South~~
19. Montana	44.
20. Mississippi	45.
21. Michigan	46.
22. Maine	47.
23. Minnesota	48.
24. North Carolina	49.
25. South Carolina	50.

INT. BALLROOM

There's a big fund-raiser happening for kids or breast cancer or
something. A bunch of FANCY LADIES and UPTIGHT GUYS are standing
around drinking champagne and telling dirty jokes.

Suddenly a bunch of THUGS burst into the room and shoot their guns
in the air. All of the Fancy Ladies and Uptight Guys start
panicking, except for CHARLES. He knows exactly what he has to do.
Good thing he brought his BALLPOINT PEN.

He pulls it out of his pocket and throws it across the room, hitting
a power box and killing the lights.

                    THUG #1
              Hey, what's going on?!

WOOSH *WOOSH* *THUMP* *SMACK* *FWIP* *FWIP* *FWIP* *THUMP*

                   ALL THUGS
             AGH! HEY! WHAT?! UGH!

Suddenly the lights turn back on, and all of the Thugs are dazed and
tied up and have wieners drawn on their faces.

INT. FANCY RESTAURANT

I'm on a date with a HOT BABE, *again*.

It's going really well because I'm so charming and attractive and not balding. It's clear now that the Hot Babe is gonna let me have sex with her, and honestly, I can't wait. There's nothing I would love to do more and there's no reason I might cry afterward.

EXT. BASEBALL FIELD

It's a beautiful day at the BALLPARK, and a small CROWD has gathered
to watch a BALL GAME. The HOME TEAM is in the field while the
VISITING TEAM bats. The score is something to something else, it's an
inning, and there are some outs (maybe).

BATTER #4 steps up to the plate.

                    UMPIRE
          PLAY BALL!

REMINDER: Find out if the Umpire really says that every time.

```
--------------
```

INT. LIVING ROOM

JULES is finally putting it all together.

>   JULES
> Oh my god, it all makes sense now! I knew he
> was cheating on me, I knew it! I would come
> home from work, and I could just tell someone
> had been in the bed, or that someone had just
> taken a shower, but his hair wasn't wet or
> anything. No way he just took a shower. He was
> cheating on me, and he knew I was putting it
> together. He knew I would have divorced him
> right on the spot and taken every last cent. He
> had to get rid of me to protect his money.
>   (beat)
> It was her... *she's the one who killed me*. Oh my
> god! So all I gotta do is figure out how to pin
> the murder on her and I can finally cross over!
> That's my unfinished business!
>   (beat)
> And you're gonna help me.

>   WHOOPI GOLDBERG
> Oooooh, no! I am NOT doing this again!

INT. OFFICE

PETE and KYLE are standing by the water cooler, shooting the
proverbial shit.

STACY enters, and her BOOBS look super-fuckin' sweet.

Pete and Kyle are all like, "whoa."

INT. MY WALLET

                         GEORGE WASHINGTON
            Hello? Is anyone there?

INT. MONICA AND RACHEL'S APARTMENT

MONICA and RACHEL are sitting on the couch talking about something
really boring.

PHOEBE's running around like an idiot.

KRAMER enters. What?!

EXT. RANCH

ALAN is leading a herd of cattle into the corral.

His eldest son, JACK (28), brings up the rear, assuring no strays
leave the heard. His middle son, TAYLOR (25), loads bales of hay into
the feeding troughs. While his youngest son, RILEY (19), is
apparently a "dancer" now.

EXT. DOWNTOWN LOS ANGELES - STREET

DETECTIVE BECKETT is in a high-speed car chase with a WHITE VAN full of ROBBERS (four). They're zigging and zagging through traffic, endangering the lives of INNOCENT BYSTANDERS. Detective Beckett is able to keep up with them just fine, but he knows he has to do something soon or people *will* die.

> DETECTIVE BECKETT
> Here, Rookie. Take the wheel.

The nervous ROOKIE (22, a rookie) takes the steering wheel as Beckett reaches into the backseat and grabs the ROCKET LAUNCHER. Then he rolls down his window and climbs out.

> DETECTIVE BECKETT (CONT'D)
> Keep 'er steady, rook!

> ROOKIE
> OK.

Beckett waits for a clear shot, and... WHOOSH! He hits the van dead-on, and it explodes 100 percent and goes two hundred feet into the air. Beckett climbs back into the car and brings it to a stop.

> DETECTIVE BECKETT
> (to the Rookie)
> Lesson number one: don't forget that we have
> rocket launchers.

> ROOKIE
> OK.

EXT. SHOPPING MALL - PARKING LOT

There's CARS everywhere. I'd say at least two hundred. And that
doesn't even include the ones that are either coming or going. It's
urban chaos. (good phrase, remember that)

A large CHARTER BUS pulls into the lot, and it's completely full of
OLD PEOPLE.

Uh-oh... Here we go again!

Flowers

Flowers are pretty to look at,
Flowers are pretty to smell.
But flowers given to my ex-girlfriend,
Make her say "go to hell."

Why did "Friends" work so well?
- They had fun
- They had plenty of sex (sometimes w/each other)
- Some of them were girls
    - Boobs
- They lived in New York
    - Everybody ♡s NY!
- They talked about issues (important ones)
- Chandler

INT. ABRAHAM LINCOLN'S BEDROOM

PRESIDENT ABRAHAM LINCOLN puts on his jacket and heads for the DOOR because he's going to catch a PLAY.

Suddenly there is a bunch of LOUD NOISES and flashes of LIGHT, and then, as if from thin air, JACK TRAVIS (Jason Statham) appears in the middle of the room. President Lincoln is terrified.

> JACK TRAVIS
> Listen up, Mr. President. My name is Jack Travis and I am from the future. Your life is in danger and you need to come with me *right now*.

> PRESIDENT ABRAHAM LINCOLN
> Ooh... yeah, it's just- I gotta go catch this play. Can it wait?

Jack Travis makes this face like, "good grief."

EXT. THE UNIVERSE

Huh, that's strange. THE WORLD is *not* revolving around AMY.

INT. MY BANK ACCOUNT

A TUMBLEWEED rolls by. *A TUMBLEWEED.*

You get it.

INT. DORM ROOM

STACEY is sitting at her DESK hard at work on some HOMEWORK because she is a COLLEGE STUDENT at COLLEGE.

Her roommate ANDREA enters.

> ANDREA
> Hey, Stacey. I just got these drugs from my friend Gary.

Andrea holds up a bag of DRUGS.

> ANDREA (CONT'D)
> Do you wanna do them with me and then maybe explore our sexualities?

> STACEY
> Oh, no thank you. I wanna make sure I'm super-boring when I'm older.

Andrea nods like, "Oh, that makes sense."

INT. BANK

A bunch of PEOPLE stand in a line waiting to make any number of
MONETARY TRANSACTIONS.

JOSEPH enters, and boy is he handsome. He immediately grabs the
attention of everyone he passes. Probably because he has great HAIR
and his CLOTHES fit him properly and he's got this perfect little
smile on his face that almost isn't a smile but it's definitely a
smile, ya know? He just makes you go, "Wow, look at him."

> JOSEPH
> Ladies and gentlemen, may I have your attention
> please?

Everyone turns and looks at him like, "Who's this guy?" Then he
pulls out a MACHINE GUN.

> JOSEPH (CONT'D)
> I'll be robbing you now.

Ohhhhhhh, he's a burglar.

EXT. PARK

RACHEL and MONICA are going for a jog while also having a casual conversation.

They're wearing athletic, tight-fitting TOPS, so their BOOBS look great and they're kind of bouncing a little bit.

Then... somebody breaks up with somebody? I don't know.

INT. STAN'S OFFICE

PETER sits in a CHAIR across from STAN, who sits at his DESK. Peter has a look of shock on his face.

> STAN
> You're fired, Peter. I'm sorry.

> PETER
> Are you fuckin' kiddin' me, Stan, you're firing me?! After all these years! After everything I've done for this goddamn company! Just thrown to the street like some kind of... outdated piece of equipment?! 'Cause I'm inferior technology, right? You can go out and replace me with some fancy new machine. Just let the machines take over. Is that it? Like, fuckin'... *Terminator Salvation*. Just let the machines run the world! Well guess what, Stan. Machines *don't* run the world, *people* run the world. And you know what people like and appreciate? CUSTOMER. SERVICE. You can't get that from the machines, no way. There's no customer service in *Terminator Salvation*. You see that movie? *Terrible* customer service. Because it's the fuckin' apocalypse, dude. We let the machines take over, and the whole world goes to shit! We start sacrificing quality customer service, and the next thing you know there's fuckin' Terminators around every corner just waiting to *smash* your skull in with their metal feet. *CRUUUNCH!* That's your future, Stan. All because you decided to *terminate* quality customer service.

A beat.

> STAN
> That was a really cool speech... but you're still fired—

> PETER
> I KNOW that!

INT. SCIENCE PLACE

DR. THOMPSON and his LADY ASSISTANT are very carefully doing some
SCIENCE STUFF.

>   DR. THOMPSON
>   Just one more science thing... and I'll have
>   cured cancer.

>   LADY ASSISTANT
>   Unbelievable. You really are an amazing man, Dr.
>   Thompson.

>   DR. THOMPSON
>   *Oh my god* I know that already shut the fuck up
>   for a second.

INT. CASINO

A bunch of PEOPLE are GAMBLING and DRINKING and RUINING THEIR
MARRIAGES.

DANNY OCEAN enters and he looks really cool. Then fourteen OTHER
GUYS (Brad Pitt, Casey Affleck, etc.) enter dressed like CASINO
EMPLOYEES and walk off in different directions.

NOTE: Depending on how many *Ocean's* have been made, the number of
Other Guys can change. If we're still at *Thirteen*, take one out. If
Fifteen's already been made, add one. You get it.

At least one hundred MONKEYS enter.

INT. ADOLF HITLER'S OFFICE

ADOLF HITLER sits at his desk working on his GENOCIDE.

Suddenly there is a bunch of LOUD NOISES and flashes of LIGHT and then, as if from thin air, JACK TRAVIS (Jason Statham) appears in the middle of the room. Hitler's pissed.

                    HITLER
               (in German)
          What is this?! Who the hell are you?!

                    JACK TRAVIS
          Sorry... I don't speak *dick.*

Then Jack Travis shoots Hitler in the HEAD with a GUN and his head explodes everywhere and it's awesome.

INT. LIVING ROOM

KRISTIN is doing her daily Tae Bo workout. She moves around
according to the instructions given to her by a BLACK MAN on her TV,
and she's really workin' up a good hot sweat.

Then her roommate TANYA enters with *a bunch* of SOY MILK. Probably.
Right?

EXT. HOUSE

ROY is sitting on the porch enjoying a nice cool glass of lemonade
on a beautiful summer afternoon.

An ALLIGATOR walks buy wearing a suit and carrying a BRIEFCASE. He
notices Roy and tips his CAP.

                    ALLIGATOR
          Afternoon.

Roy just stares at the Alligator in shock for a few moments; then he
remembers that he did a bunch of DRUGS a few minutes ago, so he's
like:

                    ROY
          Ohhhhhh, OK. I get it.
               (to Alligator)
          Hello, Mr. Alligator!

                    ALLIGATOR
          It's actually Dr. Alligator.

Really Cool Movie Titles

- Strictly Business
- In Your Dreams
- ~~Big Daddy~~
- Pedal To The Metal
- Punch It!
- Chicken Fight
- Take Who For A Loop?
- One In The Hand
- Addicted To Gloves
- ☆ The Peanut Butter Boys
- Peas In A Pod
   - (sci-fi)
- The Plains Of Avalon
- You Can Call Me Alf
- Nic of Time
   - (main character's name is "Nic")
- Yeah Right
- Let The Games Begin
- ~~Philadel~~
- Oh Yeah, Baby
- Baby Go Boom
- Talk About A Pickle
- A Case Of The Mondays

- Mr. Touchdown
- Mr. Homerun
- Mr. Slam Dunk
- Mrs. Slam Dunk (!)

- California Nightmarin'
   - (horror)
- Ugh, Not Again
- Friend Request Accepted
   - (horror/thriller)
- Gimme A Break ~~Already~~

INT. DINER - NIGHT

It's another quiet night at this hole-in-the-wall diner, the only customers being a few sad-looking TRUCK DRIVERS and one MYSTERIOUS MAN who sits at the counter. A WAITRESS approaches him with a POT OF COFFEE.

> WAITRESS
> More coffee, darlin'?

> MYSTERIOUS MAN
> Sure. But the name's not "darlin'."

The Mysterious Man looks up *dramatically* to reveal that he's actually:

> HARRY POTTER
> It's Potter. *Harry Potter.*

Then Harry Potter pulls out a GUN and *robs the place blind.*

NOTE: "robs the place blind" is just a figure of speech. Harry Potter will not be blind in this film.

EXT. THE WHITE HOUSE - MORNING

It's a beautiful morning in Washington, D.C.

THE PRESIDENT walks outside with a CUP OF COFFEE in his hand. He likes to take in a little fresh air each morning before he starts his day. Then he hears a strange sound and looks up into the sky.

There's a MISSILE headed straight for him.

                    THE PRESIDENT
          Ah, dang it.

BOOM. The White House is blown to *smithereens*.

INT. TERRORIST HEADQUARTERS - CONTINUOUS

All the TERRORISTS celebrate via high fives. Except for the HEAD TERRORIST, who sits perfectly still. He knows this is only beginning of the:

TITLE CARD: "BEST WAR EVER"

```
---------------
```

EXT. PARK

AMY (29, not that important) is on a walk. Then suddenly some
STEGOSAURUSES show up and start ripping her apart. They're herbivores
by nature, but they just couldn't look at her stupid ugly face for
one more second, so they ate her.

NOTE: This movie will require dinosaurs.

EXT. OUTDOOR BASKETBALL COURT

A crowd of mostly young BLACK PEOPLE stand around the court getting
"buck wild" (slang term) as nine BLACK GUYS and one WHITE GUY are on
the court playing a heated, but clean, game of 5-on-5 basketball.
And let me tell ya, the atmosphere is electric. I mean, guys are
dunking, and *dribbling*, and *behind the back passing* and just overall
"balling" (slang term).

                         WHITE GUY
          Here you go, ball! Ball, ball! Ball, ball, ball!

But he doesn't get the ball 'cause he's a "buster" (slang term?).

INT. BEDROOM

GEORGE and BETH are engaging in some sensual foreplay that we can
only assume will lead to cool sex.

George squeezes her LEFT BOOB for a little bit, then her RIGHT BOOB
for a little bit. Then he squeezes both boobs at the *same time*.
Sweet. Then Beth's like, "Oh yeah? Watch this." And she puts her hand
down his pants and touches his WIENER a bunch! *Sweet.* So George is
like, "Oh yeah?!" And he does that thing where you take someone's
nose and show it to them.

                    GEORGE
          Got your nose!

Sweet?

INT. CLEOPATRA'S PRIVATE BATH HOUSE (BATHROOM?)

CLEOPATRA is taking a MILK BATH and she's really into it.

Suddenly there is a bunch of LOUD NOISES and flashes of LIGHT, and then, as if from thin air, JACK TRAVIS (Jason Statham) appears in the middle of the room. Cleopatra is startled to say the least.

> JACK TRAVIS
> (so sexy)
> Mind if I join you?

Cleopatra makes this face like, "Uhhhh, *no I don't!*"

INT. BOWLING ALLEY

A bunch of FAT SLOBS are BOWLING. This one Fat Slob, JOEY, is the best and everyone knows it. He's just throwing one STRIKE after another, and EVERYONE ELSE is watching him and cheering.

STEVE "STRIKEMAN" JACKSON enters. Everyone gasps.

> PERSON #1
> That's Strikeman Jackson! He's the best champion that ever lived!

> PERSON #2
> Strikeman Jackson? I thought he retired!

> PERSON #1
> I guess not.

> PERSON #3
> Who the hell cares, *Strikeman's back!*

REMINDER: Think of a better nickname than "Strikeman." That's *fairly* stupid.

EXT. A PERFECT WORLD

Scoliosis is considered "really cool."

INT. OR EXT. WHEREVER.

Some PEOPLE are doing some STUFF.

Then some OTHER PEOPLE show up and they're like:

> OTHER PEOPLE
> Hey. Stop doing that stuff.

And the first People are like:

> PEOPLE
> Excuse me?! You can't tell us what to do!

Then they just kinda go back and forth like that for a while and, ya know, it's pretty interesting. But then, it starts to get really crazy and it looks like all is lost. But then, some resolution happens. And everybody's like, "phew."

I mean so overall it's gonna be a *really* good movie.

INT. FANCY RESTAURANT

ASHLEY and NICK are on their first date. Nick seems really nervous. Probably because he thinks Ashley is just the most beautiful woman in the whole wide world.

Meanwhile, Ashley does not seem nervous. Probably because she thinks Nick is boring and ugly and stupid and probably listened to *way too much* John Mayer in college.

What Dreams May Come
Last night I dreamt a dream.
A dream to end all dreams.
There was no war,
There was no black or white.
There was no religion.
There was no wrong or right.
And just when I thought,
it couldn't get any better.
Hitler shows up with Eddie Vedder.
The Pearl Jam guy.

☆Reminder:
end this one
~~better.~~ ☆

Velocicopper Tag Lines
- "They're too extinct for this shit."
- "The land before time... and C4."
- "Dinosaurs. Carnivores. Cops."
- "They're not birds YET."

Character Names
- Captain Gruff
- McMastadon
- "Scales" Detective Scales
- "Spike"
- McTeeth
- "Stretch" McLongneck
- "Flat Face" McFlat
- Hornsby
- McMeany (bad guy)
- Herb E. Vore
  - Herbie Vore

INT. MY OFFICE

I'm interviewing BRAD PITT for a potential role in my upcoming HIT
FILM and my HAIR looks better than his.

> ME
>
> Look, it's nothing personal, I just don't think
> you're right for the role, B-rad.

> BRAD PITT
>
> Oh, come on man, please! I really need this. I
> wanna be in your movie so bad! Like, *so bad*.
> You are the best. You're so good at making
> movies and I am literally desperate to be in
> one. *Please*.

I think for a moment then sigh.

> ME
>
> All right.

Brad Pitt is so excited he falls backwards in his CHAIR and gets
super-embarrassed because he's so insecure.

EXT. CEMETERY

It's raining.

TROY CARTER stands next to a COFFIN with a few other people around
him. The contents of the coffin? His dead wife Melissa.

An unmarked car pulls up next to the funeral. Troy notices the car.
He tries to see who's in the car, but the windows are tinted.
Something's not right; he's seen that car before. The tension builds
a bunch as we cut back and forth between Troy's face looking at the
car and the car.

Then a bunch of DOVES fly in front of the car, and once they're
clear, Troy sees the window roll down just enough for someone to
stick a GUN out the window. It's MCMAHON (the bad guy).

                    TROY
          Everybody *down*!

Troy pushes some OLD LADY to the ground right as the bullets start
flying. He dives over the coffin containing his dead wife Melissa and
pulls out his matching GOLD PISTOLS and starts firing at the car.

                    MCMAHON
               (facetiously)
          I just came to pay my respects!

BANG *BANG* *BANG* *BANG* *BANG* *BANG* *BANG* (gunshots)

INT. CASTLE OF KRIBERIA

Various PEASANTS and SLAVES walk throughout the castle completing
any number of daily TASKS.

KING GREGARIOUS is on a casual walk with his son LEONUS.

                    KING GREGARIOUS
          Someday, Leonus, this entire kingdom will be
          yours.

                    LEONUS
          OK, yeah, cool. But what if, like,
          hypothetically, I wanted to be, I don't know... a
          poet or a dancer or something? *Hypothetically!*

INT. LIVING ROOM

                    JONATHAN
I'm sorry, son. I know I don't deserve it, but
I'd just really like to be a part of your life.

                    BRIAN
Oh, well sorry, Pops, a little too late for
that! Where were you when I really needed you,
huh?! Where were you when I was just a young,
lonely, hungry child that needed nothing more
than the loving touch and stern guidance of a
father figure, huh? Where were you then?!

Jonathan doesn't know what to say.

                  BRIAN (CONT'D)
Where were you when I started getting boners in
fifth grade and I literally had no fucking idea
what the hell was happening to me? I was
terrified! I didn't know what a boner was! And
there was no adult male in my life that I felt
comfortable asking what was happening to my
wiener. I thought I was an alien or a mutant or
something. Because my wiener was growing and
getting harder. I thought I had a really weird
superpower or something. Like I could maybe...
use it as a weapon to fight crime. And I had to
live with that really stupid idea in my head for
years because you weren't there to tell me that
it was just a boner and everybody gets boners.
It's totally natural, it's for sex.
       (beat)
So no thanks, Dad. I don't really need you in my
life now. Because I already know what boners
are for. Thanks for nothin'.

EXT. STREET

DETECTIVE BROADWAY walks down the street. He's wearing the coolest
SHADES you've ever seen. They're perfect for his face. And his hair?
Amazing. Just flowing in the wind. He's wearing a suit, but he doesn't
look like a "Suit," you know what I mean? He just looks good. Maybe a
little too good...

He pulls a DETONATOR out of his pocket and pushes the RED BUTTON.

BOOM! The BANK behind him explodes but he barely reacts and just
keeps walking, so I guess he's a terrorist now...

```
---------------
```

EXT. YANKEE STADIUM

It's a beautiful day at Yankee Stadium as the Baltimore Orioles are in town.

Bottom of the fourth, one out. DEREK JETER steps up the plate. First pitch, and... CRACK! He hits it deep to right field. The right fielder runs back as fast as he can, but it doesn't matter as the ball goes over the fence for a HOME RUN and hits AMY (29, dumb idiot) in the head and kills her.

EXT. PARKING LOT

JASON pulls up in his STUPID CAR and parks.

Then he gets out and puts on his STUPID JACKET and even STUPIDER
SUNGLASSES.

Then a COP shows up and arrests him for being THE WORST.

INT. RESTAURANT

It's Friday night, and TIFFANY, GRACE, and RITA are getting their proverbial "drink on" in an attempt to forget about how miserable their day-to-day lives are. You can tell they're having a really good time because they are literally letting their HAIR down.

The WAITER approaches.

                    WAITER
          Can I get you ladies anything else?

                    TIFFANY
          Ooh! Yes. Could I get a decent man with a stable
          career, please?

Then they all laugh so hard that they start crying uncontrollably. On account of the laughter.

INT. MY OFFICE

I'm talking to superstar celebrity JENNIFER ANISTON about
potentially being in my next MAJOR MOTION PICTURE.

>   ME
>   Now, there are some nude scenes. Are you
>   comfortable with that?

>   JENNIFER ANISTON
>   (coyly)
>   What do you think?

Then Jennifer Aniston takes off her SHIRT, and her BOOBS look so
awesome I'm just like, "whoa."

INT. LIVING ROOM

A YOUNG BOY sits on the COUCH watching a baseball game, but he looks
confused. Probably because he's never met his real dad, so there's no
male role model in his life to explain how baseball works. If he
understood irony, he'd probably say something like:

            YOUNG BOY
      Thanks, Dad.

EXT. A PERFECT WORLD

YASMINE BLEETH actually returns my calls.

Music!

Cool bands to make movies about

- Aerosmith (duh)
- The Oakridge Boys
- Nirvana (too sad?)
- Pearl Jam (too boring?)
- En Vogue

(potential) Musicals

- The Chicago fire
- Cowboys (in general) (already been done?)
- dogs and/or cats
- Basketball
- ☆ - Starbucks (inception of: Seattle, etc.)
- The Internet (Bill Gates?)
- Sandwiches. food in general. Subway???

INT. CHURCH

There is a small group of PEOPLE in the church attending a FUNERAL.
One of the People is TROY CARTER, who sits in the front row because
the funeral is for his dead wife Melissa.

Suddenly the doors fly open and everyone turns around. For a few
seconds there's nothing but sunlight coming through the doors and
everyone's confused. Then all of sudden: DOVES. A bunch of 'em. And
right behind them? MCMAHON (the bad guy)!

                    TROY
          Everybody DOWN!

Troy pushes an OLD LADY to the ground and runs up to his wife's
COFFIN as McMahon tries to shoot him. Troy dives over the coffin,
knocking it over in the process. And guess what falls out of it?
Nope, not his dead wife Melissa, but a bunch of GUNS. Also a few
DOVES. Troy knew McMahon would try to hit him at his wife's funeral,
where he's most vulnerable! He grabs his matching GOLD PISTOLS and
starts shooting at McMahon, who didn't expect Troy to have those
guns in the coffin, so he has to duck behind a DIFFERENT OLD LADY,
who gets shot and dies.

                    MCMAHON
               (shouting)
          Whoa, look who's learning! Very good, Carter!

                    TROY
               (also shouting)
          Thank you!

INT. OFFICE

DEBORAH is up to her jugs in PAPERWORK.

PHIL approaches with a DOUGHNUT in each hand.

Deborah has this look on her face like, "Oh man, I want one of those." But Phil's got this look on his face like, "Nope."

                    DEBORAH
          Suck my dick, Phil.

INT. STARBUCKS

I'm sitting at a TABLE trying to write my screenplay, and let's just say, "I should have gone to business school."

A MAN enters and he has a STUPID HAIRCUT. So I stare at him for a while.

Then I grow old and die.

THE END.

INT. RESTAURANT

It's your average restaurant on your average day. Complete with some average PEOPLE enjoying some average FOOD and drinking some *very* average COFFEE.

JASON STATHAM'S CHARACTER enters with a BABY under his arm.

> WAITRESS
> Hi! Just the two of you?

Then he pulls out a GUN and points it at her.

> JASON STATHAM'S CHARACTER
> (super-cool)
> Better make it three.

WOLVERINE enters *dramatically*.

EXT. BEACH - AFTERNOON

It's a beautiful day at the beach. Everyone is having a really great
time throwing FRISBEES, dancing to radio hits, and swimming in the
cool waters of the OCEAN.

All the BABES have great BUTTS and BOOBS, and all the DUDES have
well-defined MUSCLES.

Little do they know, they're about to get attacked to death by the
SHARK PEOPLE.

EXT. MY BUTT

A FART exits.

EXT. STREET - NIGHT

It's raining. Heck, it's pouring. And honestly, somewhere in the world, an old man is snoring. Let's not kid ourselves.

TODD stands on the corner just gettin' drenched 'cause he doesn't have an umbrella. He's one of those "idiots" everyone keeps talking about.

Finally the BUS arrives and the door opens.

                    BUS DRIVER
          Sorry, no idiots allowed.

                    TODD
          Cool. I get it.

The bus drives away

EXT. BASKETBALL COURT

Four PALS are casually shooting HOOPS. You can tell they're pals because they're laughing and smiling and they're really sharing the BALL well.

>   PAL #1
> So what do guys usually talk about when they
> shoot hoops together?

>   PAL #2
> I don't know, their wives?

>   PAL #3
> Yeah. Or sex, probably. Right?

>   PAL #2
> Oh yeah, sure. Sex.

>   PAL #1
> OK, OK...
>   (beat)
> So... do you guys have sex with your wives?

REMINDER: Make friends.

INT. SCIENCE LAB

WILLIAM is hard at work on a FORMULA (the liquid variety). He looks
terrible, and he's clearly been at it all night. He combines a PURPLE
LIQUID with a GREEN LIQUID and it makes a BROWN LIQUID(?). Then he
holds that LIQUID real close to his FACE and smiles a very *devious
smile*.

                    WILLIAM
          I've done it...
               (beat)
          Liquid cancer.

Oh yeah, he's an evil scientist, by the way.

Science Fiction

What are some of the elements of great science fiction?

How did they do "Ghost?"

- Space
- Other planets
- Aliens (peaceful or violent)
- Cool Astronaut guys
- Scary Monsters (deadly, strong, large)
- Multiple dimensions (at least 2)
☆ - Time travel (consequences?)
- Transformations via Science
   - i.e., experiments
- Robots (advanced ones)
- future stuff (cars, guns, clothes, etc.)

can you have sex in space? or do you need gravity?
☆ maybe better without ☆

Zero G Spot

INT. MY OFFICE

I'm hard at work on my next BOX OFFICE HIT.

My assistant MAGGIE enters.

> MAGGIE
> Tom Cruise here to see you, sir.

> ME
> Ugh. Tell him I'm out.

EXT. COFFEE SHOP

It's a beautiful afternoon, and LAURA and STEVE are enjoying two separate CUPS OF COFFEE while also reminiscing about the good ole days when they were SCIENTISTS together in a LAB.

>   LAURA
>   It's so nice to catch up like this!

>   STEVE
>   Yes, I agree. I just wish Joe was here with us...

>   LAURA
>   I miss him too. But he made his choice and he's
>   a super-villain now. There's nothing we can do
>   about it.

>   STEVE
>   What if I told you there *was* something we could
>   do about it...

Then Steve pulls out the GEM OF DESTINY, and Laura gets this look on her face like, "omg you *didn't*."

EXT. FRONT YARD

JOHN is having a catch with his son, DANNY (9). So, basically, John throws the ball, a baseball, to Danny. Sometimes he catches it, sometimes he doesn't. Either way, eventually Danny has the ball and he throws it back to John, his dad. Then they just kinda do that back and forth for a while until Danny's like:

> DANNY
> Dad, can we stop?

> JOHN
> (taunting)
> *"Dad, can we stop?"* Fuck you, throw the ball.

EXT. VENICE CANALS

Two really cool BOATS speed through the canals side by side, barely avoiding other boats full of ITALIANS.

One of the boats is being driven by MR. BROWN, while the other one is full of INTERNATIONAL CRIMINALS (three). The Criminals keep trying to pull close to Mr. Brown's boat so one of them can jump onto it and beat him up, but they keep having to avoid some of the other boats I mentioned earlier.

Mr. Brown knows he's outnumbered, but he has an idea. He waits for them to try to get close again, and then he rams into them really hard, sending all three Criminals flying out of the boat and into a wall that smashes their heads in, causing instant death.

Mr. Brown smiles.

EXT. A PERFECT WORLD

I didn't get that BONER during PE in seventh grade.

EXT. BASKETBALL COURT

Four PALS are casually shooting HOOPS. You can tell they're pals
because they're laughing and smiling and they're really sharing the
BALL well.

> PAL #1
> Hey, guys, conversation?

> PAL #2
> Uh... conversation?

> PAL #1
> Well, I mean... conversation.

> PAL #2
> Oh, conversation.

> PAL #1
> Yeah.

> PAL #3
> Well I mean, in my opinion, conversation.

> PAL #1
> Oh, OK. I see your point.

REMINDER: Seriously, gotta make those friends.

EXT. MY MANSION

It's like the biggest HOUSE you've ever seen, and I paid for it with all the MONEY I made from my numerous HIT FILMS. I'm sitting on the porch enjoying a COLD ONE and looking off in the distance, completely content in life.

Then my close personal friend JASON STATHAM pulls up in a really cool CAR. He's wearing an awesome LEATHER JACKET, and we are just so happy to see each other 'cause we're best friends and we both have great MUSCLES.

INT. MOVIE THEATER

KEVIN and PATRICIA are on their third date, and they're watching a
ROMANTIC COMEDY. They're snuggled up to each other and sharing a
BUCKET of POPCORN and it's super-cute and Kevin can kind of see down
her shirt and he likes what he sees.

Then something funny happens in the movie and Kevin laughs at it,
but it's a really weird laugh, so Patricia makes this face like, "Eh,
I don't think this is gonna work out."

INT. SECRET HIDEOUT

All the MUTANTS are just kinda hanging out, killing time, "chilling," if you will.

Suddenly MAGNETO enters *dramatically*. Everybody stops what they're doing and turns and looks at him. 'Cause it's Magneto, ya know? Magneto shows up, you drop what you're doing. Case closed. That's like rule number one of being a Bad Mutant. He looks around for a moment and finds two METAL PIPES on the ground. Then he picks them up with his mind and bends them into a 6 and a 9.

                    MAGNETO
          Sixty-nine.

                ALL THE MUTANTS
          Yes./Dude, *tight!*/See that's why I'm not an
          X-Man, right there.

Magneto has *the best* goofs. Hands down.

EXT. TALL BUILDING

A bunch of BAD GUYS are on the sixth floor shooting their GUNS at some COPS on the ground that are hiding behind their COP CARS and are *very* scared.

The CHIEF OF POLICE grabs the MEGAPHONE and tries to say something to the Bad Guys, but it doesn't work. He tries again, nothing. He tries a couple more times, but still can't figure it out. Then he gets shot and dies.

All the other Cops are like, "Wanna get outta here?"

INT. GUNTHER'S APARTMENT

GUNTHER is sitting in a CHAIR.

ROSS, CHANDLER, JOEY, RACHEL, MONICA, and PHOEBE do not enter.
Probably because they're busy doing literally anything else.

                    GUNTHER
          I wish I had...
               (straight to camera)
          Friends.

INT. LOS ANGELES INTERNATIONAL AIRPORT

The airport is full of TRAVELERS either coming or going.

All of a sudden you see ME, like, WHOOSH! I'm running through the
terminal as fast as I can. I'm bobbin' and weavin' and jumpin' over
trash cans and my HAIR looks great. Nothin's gonna slow me down.
Then, finally, I make it: TERMINAL 78.

I run to the window just as the plane is starting to pull away. I
quickly scan the windows until... there she is, AMY. She looks over
and actually sees me! Unbelievable. I put my hand on the glass; she
does the same. We make eye contact one last time, then... I click a
red button on a DETONATOR and the plane *EXPLODES ALL OVER THE PLACE.*

Oops... (jk)

ELMO HORROR FILM

- Please Don't Kill Me Elmo
- Murderous Rage Elmo
- Serial Killer Elmo
- See you In Hellmo ☆

- rights issue ???

Teddy Roosevelt Biopic

- who could play Roosevelt?
  - Robin Williams
  ★ - Brian Dennehy
     - still alive? hopefully.

Vice President?

- Figure out what the 1900's were like ('01-'09)
- Love interest?
- Greatest Achievements
- Famous Quotes
- Teddy Bear

INT. A HALL (LIKE A BANQUET HALL, NOT A HALLWAY)

MATTHEW stands at a PODIUM in front of a panel of OLD STIFFS.

                   MATTHEW
Ladies and gentlemen, I stand before you today
humbled. One might say I've been served a
rather healthy slice of humble pie. With some
whipped cream on top and a cold glass of milk
to wash it down. Heck, I ate it up so fast I
even went back for seconds! I mean, if no one
else is gonna eat it, I sure will! I've never
been one to let pie go to waste, and I'm not
about to start just because it's a metaphor for
my failures as a man and as a student at this
fine institution. But in my shame I believe I
have learned the most valuable lesson I could
possibly learn. What lesson is that? I'll tell
you. College... is important. College is a place
to grow as a person. A place to develop the
kind of professional, but more importantly *life,*
skills that you will need to survive and find
happiness in this world. And despite the fact
that our actions while at the Kappa Kappa Gamma
house have led to my expulsion and the deaths
of thirty-seven of my fellow students, I believe
I have finally gained those very skills. I
believe I finally know how to find happiness.

                 OLD STIFF #1
And how is that, Mr. Olson?

                   MATTHEW
Well, sir, if it's all the same to you... I'm
gonna make some pie.

Matthew exits to a standing ovation.

INT. BRITNEY'S APARTMENT

It's a girl's apartment, so there's GIRL STUFF *everywhere*. Including but not limited to: FLOWERS, FRAMED PICTURES of COFFEE BEANS, a bunch of FRENCH WORDS, and of course, a PICTURE COLLAGE of all of her UGLY FRIENDS.

BRITNEY enters... and gets her period? I don't know.

INT. SOME KINDA SUPER-SECRET GOVERNMENT BUILDING OR SOMETHING

A bunch of SCIENTISTS stand around mixing STUFF and looking at THINGS.

PRESIDENT DAKOTA FANNING enters.

EXT. COLLEGE CAMPUS

It's a very old campus. All the BUILDINGS are small, and they are
made of BRICK because it's a very old campus.

Various CO-EDS walk up and down the sidewalk, most likely on their
way to class. Except for six young FRAT GUYS, who are on a streak.
We know this because we can see their PENISES and BUTTS.

INT. HIGH SCHOOL HALLWAY

EVERY SINGLE GIRL is way too confident. All of the BOYS are getting
uncontrollable boners.

DARREN enters wearing a STUPID HAT.

INT. MY BEDROOM - AFTERNOON

I'm taking another one of my trademark NAPS. And let me tell ya
what, it is going great.

EXT. THE REST OF THE WORLD - CONTINUOUS

Other ADULTS my age are leading successful and fulfilling lives.

CONCLUSION

So there you have it! That's the end of the book. Those were all of my best ideas. Pretty good, right? I could totally come up with a bunch more too. Like, at least a hundred. So if you happen to be some kind of Hollywood executive or big-time movie producer, just email your proposals to cwisthecoolest@gmail.com. And be sure to include how many millions you're offering. Twenty would be perfect.

Thanks,
C. W.